for Nelson

About us/who we are

We believe in cooperation, collaboration, and conversation.
We don't need to be rescued, tolerated, nor understood.
This is no manifesto, no call to arms.
This is a song, a dance, a movement of many colours.
What we do cannot be contained, tamed, or erased.
We shall have what we want, and we are already beautiful.
Spells cast with biros, our mouths shaping sound,
we orbit boundless love, feel this earth and our tiny gods.
We build worlds with words, our minds blossoming dirt and galaxies.
All we need is you to complete the journey home.
Join us and we shall live splendour, our lives blessed with each other.
The future we build is forever collapsing; in the gaps between our believing is where we shall find one another.

Writing was never meant to stay printed on the page.
It prowls the streets, and Public Menace is starting a riot.

www.publicmenacepoetry.com

Instagram= publicmenace20
twitter= PublicMenace8
facebook= @publicmenacepoetry

PUBLIC MENACE anthology
ISSUE #1
[the world we WANT is us]

[POETRY IS IN THE STREETS]

The World We Want Is Us: Public Menace Poetry Anthology
By Molly Beale

First published in this edition by Egg Box Publishing 2021
Part of UEA Publishing Project
Editorial copyright © **Molly Beale** 2019
International © 2021 retained by individual authors and artists.

The right of **Molly Beale** to be identified as the Editor of this work has been asserted by them in accordance with the Copyright, Design & Patents Act, 1988.
Design and typesetting by Nigel Aono-Billson
Typeset in Silky Wonderland, Openhouse, Texturina
Printed by Swallowtail Print, Norwich
Distributed by Ingram / NBN International

This book is sold subject to the condition that it shall not, by way of trade or otherwise, be lent, resold, hired out, stored in a retrieval system, or otherwise circulated without the publisher's prior consent in any form of binding or cover other than that in which it is published and without a similar condition including this condition being imposed on the subsequent purchaser.

ISBN 978-1-913861-18-6

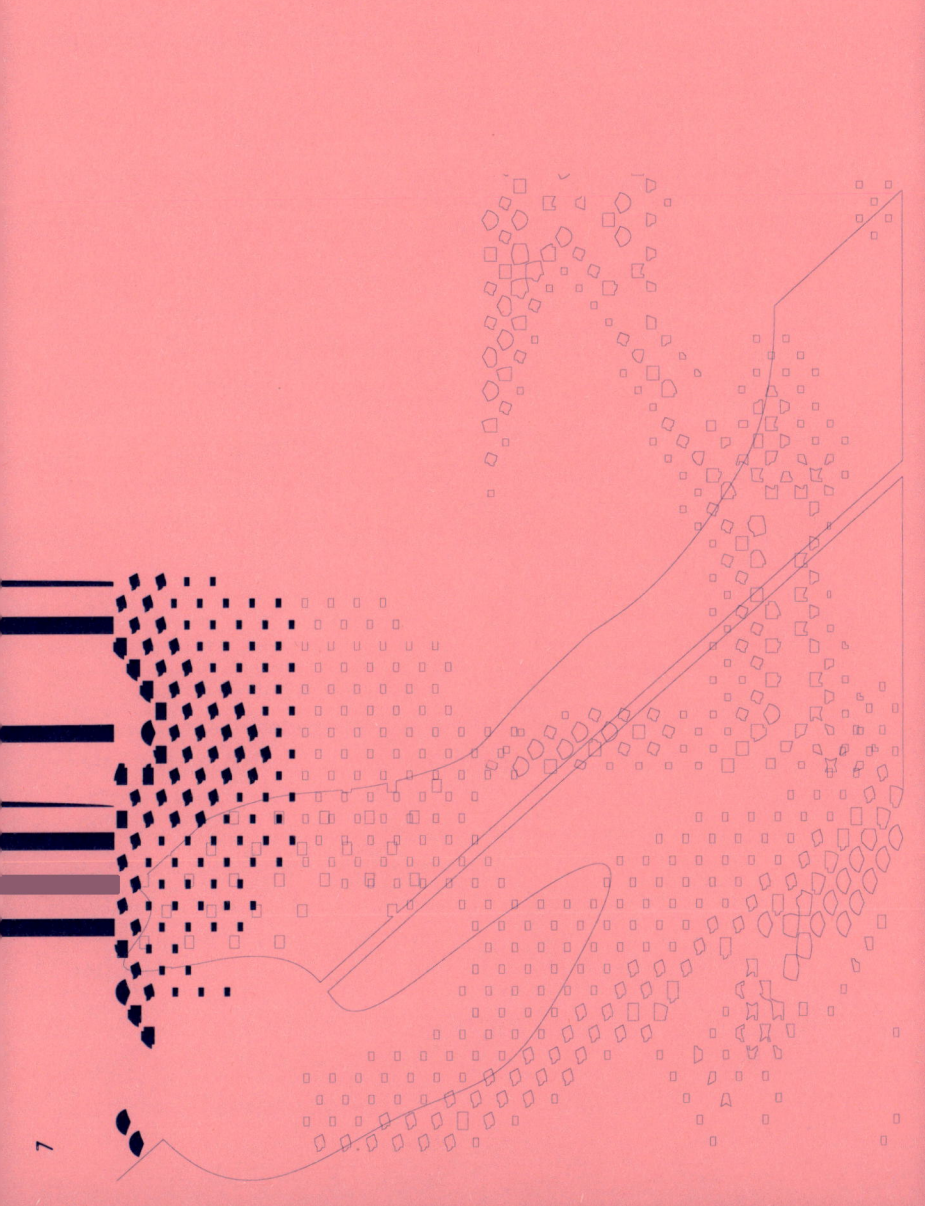

Preface

Take root among the stars
Hope
Places I've seen god
I refuse to count the grooves, arcade
Stuck in the mud
Worrier poet

Middle fingers up
New normal
Stop the killing
London in mourning (who is to blame?)
Veiled by valour
I wanted this to work so much
Why we protest
Witch hunt
The nonsonsjibhr
I hate terfs, they make me cry
Ticking time bomb
A breath of air
This developed nation
The mirror
Late night gym
Rabid doggerel
Our names are #metoo
I can't sleep

And all shall be well . . .
Some developments are unforeseeable
Song for my enemies, dedicated to my parents
Grey paint, gold pen
Lower your hammer, raise your fist/song of solidarity
To die would be an awfully big adventure
The earth rotating
The confession
Spiriting
All we have is love

Bios
Acknowledgements and Notes

	10
	14
Molly Willis	16
Ofem Ubi	17
Larry Liquid	18
Claudia Vyvyan	20
Nathan Lunt	21
	24
Ga-Modimo Dinake	26
Haziq Patel	27
Adrian Mukuvare	29
Farah	30
Meg Watts	31
Itai And Liv	33
Anna Bailey	34
John Swale	35
Plum Selfridge	36
Vitalis Gumbo	37
Sabina Redzepagic	38
David Green	39
Erica Wood	40
Kiera Summer	42
Georgie Spillman	43
Ria Bhatnagar	44
India De Bono	46
	48
Meg Watts	51
Jules Chung	52
Kiera Summer	53
Georgie Spillman	54
India De Bono	55
Bernard Tinashe Kuyayama	56
Bernard Tinashe Kuyayama	57
Ofem Ubi	58
Jesse Smith	59
	62
	68

Preface

Dear Reader,

Poetry needs people for the totality of its grace.

The same way paintings need eyes, or orchestras ears, the fine intricacies of language wrought by a singular poet cannot fulfil the circuit of sensitivity alone. Muses, editors, and readers are needed. You are essential. A reader needs other readers with whom to generate meanings; the poems we animate rely on us and how we live in our private worlds to conjure colour and depth, different and new with each person.

Whether artists or not, whether we like it or not, we're all sustained by the inherent interconnectedness of our existence. Public Menace is an attempt at joyfully celebrating the connections made possible through creating and experiencing art, and what the webs we build may bring: emotional enlightenment, learning resources, emboldened kinship, and radical togetherness.

Writing a poem will not change the world. But with whom we share the articulation of our selves, and how and what these poems inspire us to do next will bring wild futures beyond our current imagining. I hope this anthology gives people inspiration and solidarity, both creatively and otherwise: bringing us out of our discrete shells so we may best serve one another as we all fight for ourselves and each other in this crazy world we inherit.

– Molly Beale, Public Menace Editor

Trigger Warning:

The diverse poems collected here all speak without censure. Readers must be aware that this anthology contains some difficult and upsetting topics, including: transphobia, racism, misogyny, homophobia, strong language and curse words, ageism, sexual violence and assault, gendered violence, chronic illness, police brutality, death and climate catastrophe. Read and learn as you will, but please take rest and recuperation when you feel it's needed.

"WE DON'T HOLD THAT POETRY IS A FORM OF, OR REPLACES, POLITICAL ACTION. POETRY ISN'T REVOLUTIONARY PRACTISE; POETRY PROVIDES A WAY TO INHABIT REVOLUTIONARY PRACTISE, TO GROUND OURSELVES IN OUR RELATIONS TO OURSELVES AND EACH OTHER, TO THINK ABOUT AN UNEVENLY MISERABLE WORLD AND TO SPIT IN ITS FACE. . . .

WE ASSERT THAT POETRY SHOULD BE AN ACTIVITY BY AND FOR EVERYBODY."

— Andrea Abi-Karam & Kay Gabriel

> "BECAUSE WE HATE YOU AND YOUR REASON, WE INVOKE FLAMBOYANT MADNESS"
>
> — Aimé Césaire

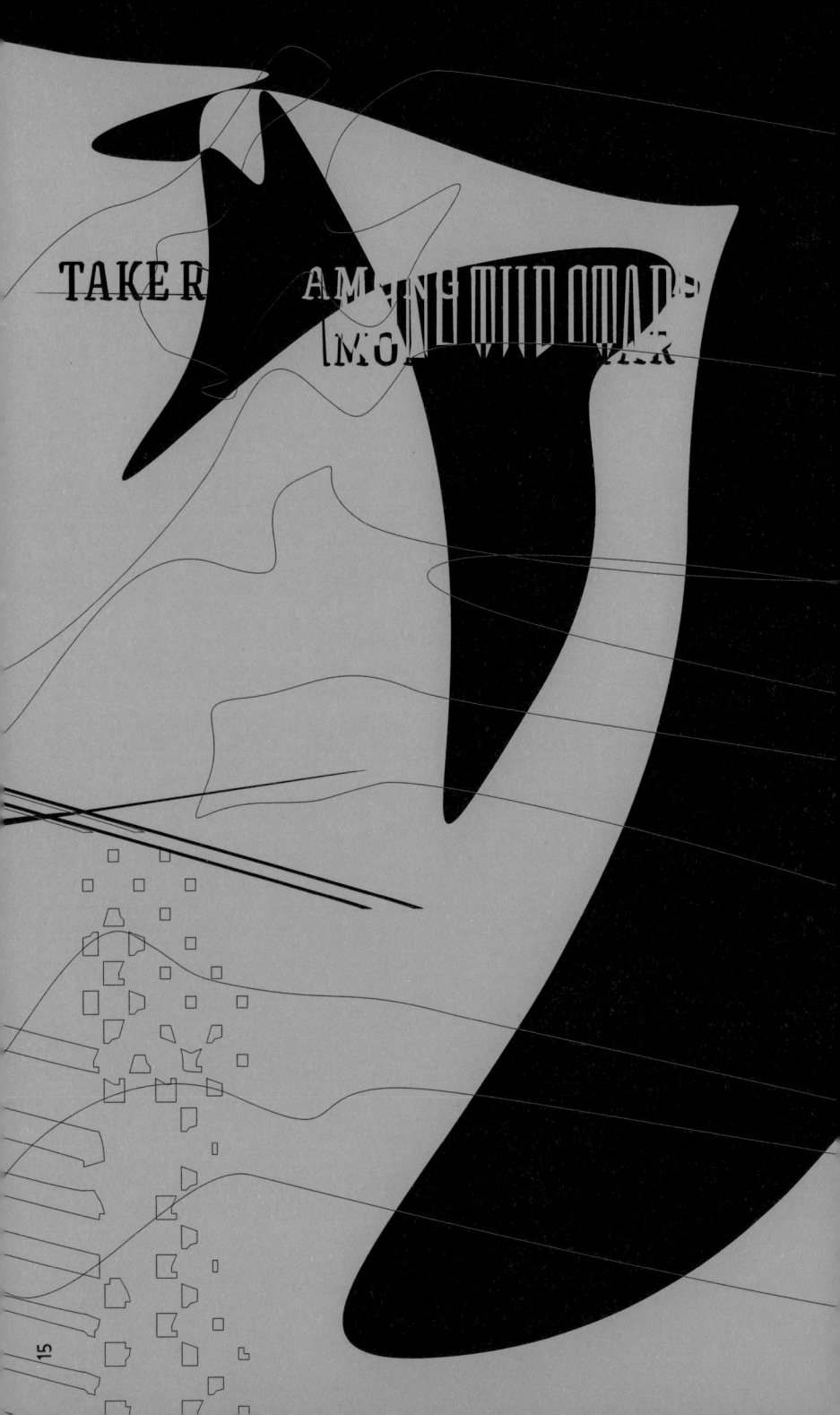

Hope
– Molly Willis

It's come to my attention that nothing really matters.
If I don't rise today, the earth will not flatten,
it will still spin on its eternal axis.

So - why would I rise today,
Or any day for that matter?
Show me the cosmic consequence of inaction.
Will God himself come to correct my infraction?
Of all the failures in the world
Why should mine matter?

A voice intervenes: *but what if,* it says.
What if there's something wonderful just up ahead?
Hope's a naive, illogical, desperate cretin
that doubles as life's most reliable weapon.

Hope's a dangerous adversary to reason
when reason declares there's no point.
Hope's a menace to systems relying on
devoid subjects.

There was no reason to march on the first day
people learned of marching.

Yet together
they gathered.
For things gain meaning
when each step matters.

Places I've seen god
– Ofem Ubi

in no particular order of wonder:

a lunatic's sermon
the stench of a drunk
truth dressed up in
toxication, rusting
coins tossed away.

in fumes
strolling across sky
pacing homeless breaths
a nomad in search of settling
harmattan dust.

in a widow's rage, a beggar's voice
a mother's knees
a baby's clenched fist
triumphantly riding the tears of a spine.
stretched out in maps on faces
yet enclosed in tribal marks.
the mouth of the dumb

echoing through lungs
a silent scream sifting through
aching to be heard.

in the eye of the blind
craving to be seen.

galloping through potholes
a splash of mud kissing
the hem of alloy wheels.

in the dark lines of a father's palm
a lightning streak racing across
thighs.

in the body of a child
camouflaged with sweat.

I refuse to count the grooves, arcade
— Larry Liquid

i refuse to count the grooves
immediate danger in instalments of four
    tell me when to love
and tell me if i'm doing it wrong

   my bed reads
i am among

      ,, symbols of deception
skilled at looking away

  a very shiny watch under some very thin ice

take the blame as it's all they give

nothing to do but everything

and make the pieces of string
     undetermined
  come over when the rubble loses its scent

   all the dreams in which the ground gives
way i am in an office

a weak batch of ecstasy and
the turmeric under my nails makes them look stale and
luminous

it never feels like it will happen until it does
  i don't think i'd know what to say
when they bombard me with the measurements
    of an after i can't afford to lose
i chase the present i hide from in my
past
    half of this prayer
summoned onstage as a laugh track
  i peep as still as possible

then move my arms by accord

this sadness is a fading flavour
    a sunset we will build with lego blocks

and i portray a strong beam
under an external current
    waiting for the next one

Stuck in the mud
– Claudia Vyvyan

I'm stuck in the mud.
I can't escape without losing my shoes,
I'll lose my leg if I try to move.
I'm sinking while screaming for help,
Offering solutions to myself.
Oil seeps into my blood but still,
I'm stuck in the mud.

My tomorrow is
Burning
Lying
Protesting and dying.
My tomorrow is stuck in the mud.

My tomorrow is
Sinking
Drowning
Sea levels rising.
My tomorrow is stuck in the mud.

My tomorrow is
Moving
Losing
No one's approving.
My tomorrow is stuck in the mud.

I'm stuck in the mud.
I can't escape without losing my shoes,
I might lose a leg if I try to move.
I'm sinking while screaming for help,
Offering solutions to myself.
Oil is seeping into my blood but still,
I'm stuck in the mud.

Worrier Poet
– Nathan Lunt

I fancy myself a warrior poet,
defiantly fighting society's ills,
vanquishing villains with
lyrical brilliance,
skewering foes with the tip of a quill.

Really... I'm more of a worrier poet,
expressing distress at the problems I see,
as much as I wish I could write righteousness
most of the time I don't think I succeed.
There's a need to address the contemporary zeitgeist,
I try to tackle the topics on trend,
but the endless succession of daily depression
suggests that the world's too broken to mend.

What good is a poem to punish injustice
when trust in the heart of humanity dies?
Why try to fight back against creeping corruption
when honesty's enemies choke it with lies?
Is it purely delusion to think that a poet
can sway peoples' spirits with just the right words;
as if some combination of miracle syllables
might hold the secret to saving our world?

There're people who tell me I'm wasting my efforts,
that nothing will ever get better than this:
if something is broken, it's broken forever,
and just getting by is as good as it gets.

Should I remain silent,
not write about violence,
political liars and government sins?
When I think I should quit,
I remind myself this;
when good people do nothing
then evil still wins.

Yes, the future may seem
quite abysmally bleak,
that won't change with a few lines of verse...
But I'd rather campaign,
even if it's in vain-
resignation is worse.

It's too easy to stay feeling down and defeated,
repeating the same empty mantras of change.
But I won't accept things will never get better,
not whilst a shred of hope still remains.

So, bring me a banner emblazoned with slogans
I'll shout out a poem and join in the march,
I'll channel my worries to something creative
I'll fight with the flames of a warrior's heart.

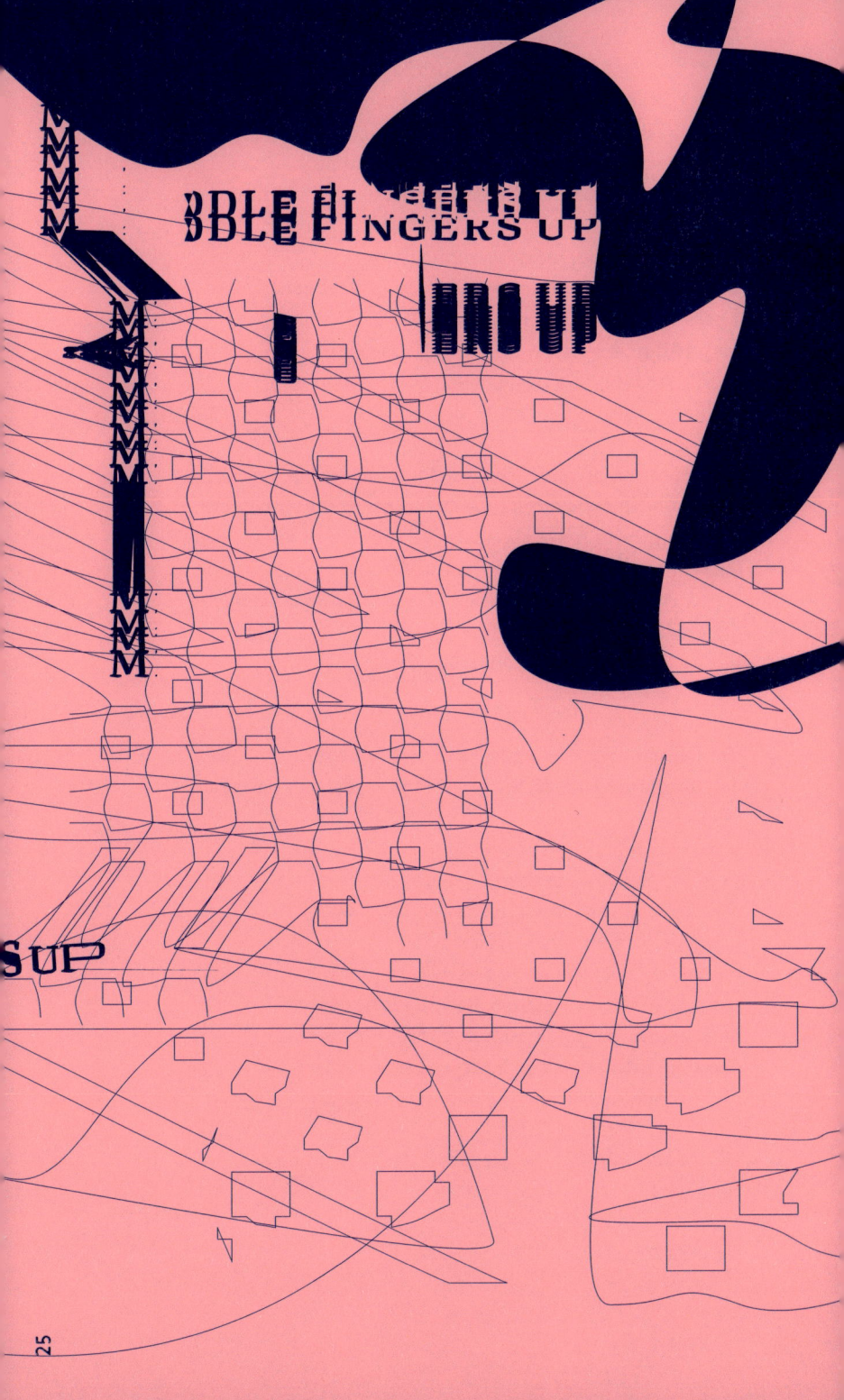

New normal
– Ga-Modimo Dinake

An x-ray view of what was before whilst looking for the after now
a resurrection and afterlife, some biblical prophecy.
Be aware of the consciousness under attack by malware
soon to fully develop a spyware. Your mentality
your software operating system
needs an upgrade. This virus just gave a reboot.
There's a simple task manager
for putting on a mask; betterment of the self
a daily update. The past is what you have lived
it all crashed.

Our attention on affection
hacked, scanned everyday as we usher in the cyborg era.
Some lifestyles must abort; social interaction digitalized
friends are strangers on social media. Here:
the birth of social distancing... Can't we see the danger!?
People have become invisible.
But, let's put aside propaganda,
it's not in this agenda.

In uncertain atmospheres dwells fear of change
a wave of intolerance, the dominant experience a sense
of grief.

Fragments of blame echo
chambers of escalation: issues on face masks, the colour of skin
being policed by empty leaders.
The pandemic took a 360 degree turn
to make a worldwide web. Coming full circle
back to localisation, national budget
personal introspection. Everyone is loading
their data refreshed on the page of the mind.

Before handshakes, people kissed to greet.
Here we tap our feet gathering
the tone of joy. Togetherness a remedy
for memory.

Stop the killing
– Haziq Patel

Stop the killing
Stop the slaughter
How many murders under police order?

Stop the killing
Stop the slaughter
We want justice for our sons and daughters.

Society rigged, depriving us bread,
Yet man cuffed gonna end up dead.
Babylon's foot pressed on our necks
Topping our folk getting far ahead.
No matter what you do, fight for the truth.
Gotta rise up, fists pumped over our heads.

Stop the killing
Stop the slaughter
How many murders under police order?

Stop the killing
Stop the slaughter
We want justice for our sons and daughters.

Them say 9 9 9 for emergency
But we get 6 6 6 for B A M E.
Minorities oppressed through authority,
Crimes they commit with impunity.
Police officers have immunity,
Free to terrorize our community.

Stop the killing
Stop the slaughter
How many murders under police order?

Stop the killing
Stop the slaughter

We want justice for our sons and daughters.

No justice! No peace! We hail through the streets,
We get on our knees,
Still ya ignore our pleas.
We march we shout we protest,
Police batons smashing our heads.
Ya cry for your cities burning
But can't shed a tear for our dead.
Coz ya colour blind ya only see white,
We gotta tear up the root the branch
Remove this blight.

Stop the killing
Stop the slaughter
How many murders under police order?

Stop the killing
Stop the slaughter
We want justice for our sons and daughters.

Remember Oluwale in 69,
1000s buried since that time,
Lapita Douglas Cole Rigg Alder
Blackstock Sylvester Sey Gardner.
Too many to name
How many more crimes?
Yet ya nah gonna find police serving time,
Systems corrupt so we gotta erupt.
Watch out police, warn the feds,
I say ya can't make an omelette
without cracking some eggs.

Stop the killing
Stop the slaughter
How many murders under police order?

Stop the killing
Stop the slaughter
We want justice for our sons and daughters.

Stop the killing
Stop the slaughter
How many murders under police order?

Stop the killing. Stop the slaughter.
We want justice for our dead.

London in mourning (who is to blame?)
– Adrian Mukuvare

'Another victim of statistics'
Another life devoured,
by the street? Another life
cut by the knife;
a life *sho(r)t*
lived. Amazing Grace
we sing *Once was blind...*
Auden's Funeral Blues
Stop all the clocks...

Who's to blame?
Another victim
has a name. It fades
into memory, a cultural
sweep under the carpet. London
turns red. Another moment of silence...

Mothers, friends, and relatives
cry living in fear.
London turns red; an open door

to campaign. Political parties promise security,
the law enforced better than ever. Breaking news.

So, who is to blame?
'Society, education system, lone parents, the government'
London mourns *Once was blind...*
Concealing the truth in our hearts,
London mourns: stop the clocks.

Veiled by valour
– Farah

For those too blind to see the writing on the wall
the ink of my soul laced with atrocities
too numerous to number & veiled
by valour: My beloved land may have been stolen,
but the sky envelopes us both & teaches;
we can co-exist in unity, equally, unanimously.
We are supported by the earth
& wider. Each other. At the moment neglected
our songs of grievance & loss.
It does not take much to iterate the thought.
A state in which all are equal is better than an apartheid state.

I wanted this to work so much
– Meg Watts

Poet's Note: This stream-of-consciousness poem essentially encapsulates my sheer frustration at Extinction Rebellion's actions in London during the October Rebellion of 2019. The five days I spent peacefully protesting left me in a state of mild-to-abject horror, whilst also unfortunately confirming my uneasiness about the movement. This poem is written for certain members of XR: the apolitical, the 'police! we love you' chanters, the ones who are disinterested in engaging with XR YOUTH seemingly because their intersectionality is a divergence from the established order. I have left it in a very raw form, as it was written in a time of very raw feeling.

'Do you feel like we've achieved something this week?'

A heavy silence, laden with the ticking of internal cogs, descends.

many sad environmentalists in many sad corners ruminate
the ineffectiveness of action the flaws in their movement; the fact
we don't have time for this.
heads bowed, eyes glazed
or nattering incessantly
insularly
within echo chambers; similar, 'fine-upstanding people'
ignoring the glaring issues, self-distracting and deluding,
dancing and gluing and hooping and locking-on
inside the runaway train
hurtling towards the poor, disadvantaged, underprivileged
FIRST-
too late.
the damage is already done.
this is not just a fight for our global future, our future children;
it's a fight for the people here and now,
who are suffering,
invisibly,
away from the idyll of your home.
these people should take precedence over those who do not yet exist.
they are living, breathing, and will not be ignored.
I ask you,
fighters-for-'our'-future:
do you see them? do you care?
are you willing to listen?

Why we protest
– Itai and Liv

When today's youth become tomorrow's leaders,
I hope for change surpassing my generation.

That every child spread their unclipped wings,
that no black child feels why the caged bird sings;
only understanding by reading, finding freedom with Ms Maya Angelou.

We protest to be heard in a world
where to the privileged
equality feels like oppression.
Life a game with more snakes than ladders,
victims of hate forced by rules they didn't create.

We protest with those who refuse to be silenced.
We speak up to unite, not divide.
But the status quo has selective hearing,
refuses to hear our plight.
Dinosaurs roam the halls of power.

Still, we march on to evoke understanding.
I wonder,
can empathy be the vanguard?
Intersectionality center stage of the postcard
I send to the marginalised. I wish we could meet here;
when I speak to all shades of humanity
look deep within:

How does it feel to be persecuted?

As a youth I asked Mamma:
'Why do some white people hate us so much?
It's as if we made them slaves.'
I hope my daughter never asks me the same.

Witch hunt
– Anna Bailey

I'm not alive enough to do more than
take up space, sharing frustration the
way trees share carbon, a secret fusion
of roots beneath the soil. The language
of the unheard sticks to your shoes,
crumbles on doormats and carpets.
There are worse things: I could ruin
the crops, steal spoons and sugar
bowls, push your neighbour off
his ladder. I could sink my
teeth into forbidden fruits.
Fix me to the ducking
stool with iron bands
lest I bite through
every rope you tie
to me. *When a*
woman thinks
alone, she
thinks
evil.

The nonsonsjibhr
– John Swale

Twas brilig not, the Nonsonsjibhr
laid last laugh maffle 'pon the stage
 lips loaded snorts to the pre cough droves
as his secret mammons again outsayed

Beware The Nonsonsjibhr England
his tongue that fogs, hands wash thems elves
of you and stay alert planned stolid
brutish common nonsense hells!

morefoold with chronic bics in claw
as ungreat grendfalls sucked your trust
to rip you as from shores before
stuff Brutish bullgods with your dust

canned laughter none! This fool be wise
lost where to cry where to guffaw?
feeds chelsea smiles as he belies
ye great unwashed germs off the floor

one two one two his nonsonsjibr
mircrophone "will test us all"
his killing joke is out of sight
in hee-haws hath the poor ones rawr

and hast thou heard the nonsonsjibhr
           come chortle round, we be allowed
saieth the house of uncommon wealth
to trust in common non sense now!

Twas brilig not, the Nonsonsjibhr
laid last laugh maffle pon the stage
 lips loaded snorts to the pre cough droves
as his secret mammons again outsayed

I hate terfs, they make me cry
– Plum Selfridge

down with the berlin wall, artificially inseminate me with
yr big ovipositor, tentacle fuck me,
slime and gunge me, wet n messy, tarred and feathered
cauled {ref:::::::::: seamus heaney, punishment}
seamus heaney says 'fuck terfs' <3 <3 [not rlly]
        Down with terf-a-bell, {ref:::::: PETER PAN}
FUCKING TERF <><> i dont believe in terfs but
They still are, they just fucking ARE<<<
They exist:::::::::::::::::::::::::::bcos
Just not believing means sweet fucking nothing just bcos
I dont believe>>>>> you still are
so fucking piss on my wig
PINK bob wig >>>> i am crying / you are a terf
And i sit and watch your face on zoom you fucking terf
Terf-a-bell, terf terf terf, terf
i dont believe in terfs i dont believe in terfs i dont believe in terfs
But they all clap and you still exist
{insert sad face emoji}

Ticking time bomb
— Vitalis Gumbo

Our country's captured carelessly
by class and race systems simultaneously;
leaders 'leading' without proper lenses
to see our scandalous spaces.

Lacking a democratic aura
promoting all people regardless, explicitly
enhancing life chances. But certainly,

there is animosity.

This time bomb is ticking
dangerously
causing myriad problems;
leaders hide from our boroughs.

Closed-door talks must be timeless
to correct the trends affecting our hearts.

Any colour: unique. Never a measure.
But what is colour without breadth?
We must maximise our talent.

Businesses blinkered by association,
profiting from blindness. Bravery's required.

The steps we take illuminate.
Our strides illustrious. Gains irreversible.
The whole process an innocuous
fusion of cultures; services rendered with humility,
thorny issues eliminated. Selfless service
propelling the country forward
to a new lease of life.

A breath of air
– Sabina Redzepagic

Basic human necessity held hostage
blackened windows never open;
days turn to weeks, months
years. This is how I picture you,
suffocating silently.

This developed nation
– David Green

In this Developed Nation, a nineteen-year-old woman sleeps in a bag in a doorway.
In this Developed Nation, a working family of four relies on the local food bank.
In this Developed Nation, grandmothers live on pittance, dying lonely.
In this Developed Nation, my friends use drugs to fill a spiritual chasm.
In this Developed Nation, stateless refugees are processed in cages.
In this Developed Nation, slave labour is abolished (still persists).
In this Developed Nation, our media patronises the lowest common denominator.
In this Developed Nation, unscrupulous employers bulldoze workers' rights.
In this Developed Nation, the population's kept divided, ineffective.
In this Developed Nation, *'I'm not a racist... but...'*
In this Developed Nation, black people are stop/searched nine times more than whites.
In this Developed Nation, under four percent of rape reports end in conviction.
In this Developed Nation, seventeen percent of adults take anti-depressants.
In this Developed Nation, suicide's the biggest killer of men under fifty.
In this Developed Nation, children cut themselves to relieve pain.
In this Developed Nation, I'm a snowflake if I care.

The mirror
– Erica Wood

Her 06:17 alarm shrieked. Conscripted to the regime:
Birth-control, bikini wax, vitamins, SlimTea,
drawing back her fringe for the prologue –
an hour of ballet. She ticked it off her list
began to imitate The Mirror's every stitch,
tug, adjustment, fiddle. Together,
they re-examined: Perhaps too exposed
too covered-up-enough skin? At guilt's nipple
she sipped only a little, fearing scales
notification: mid-season sales
painted brick-red lips, thrust a bronzer
brush upon the contours of her face:
Forehead, cheekbones, jawline, nose.
Practiced her strut, giggle, and pose-
recited the script of words to employ, those
to avoid. Mimicking The Mirror, she mumbled:

'A grocer who dreams is offensive to the buyer'

Paid the pound of flesh with
a blade to skin, possessed
seamstress in distress.
Andromeda, chained to inability:
confess, digest, refresh – alienation

in a dress. The Mirror scanned her barcode
policing the surface: pores, pimples, wrinkles
stretchmarks. Seeking praise
she performed a grin
but His lowered brow embroidered
a frown to dress her in sackcloth
ashes. Clay in His fist, He molded her
conformance to the role
she must play. Ego suppressed by Superego:
Shame is a painful birth.

Consumed by bathroom walls closing in,
her script was smothered with blank
spaces between each chewed up word.

Defiance: a salubrious mindset manifested.
Her lipstick bled onto the fogged-up mirror,
the bathroom floor, a puddle of maroon –
wine from the broken Amphora;
her cheeks, tickled pink as a Robin's breast.
Beauvoir's words reflected in her crystalline eyes:

'One is not born, but rather becomes, a woman'

Late night gym
– Kiera Summer

in warm air patchouli rises diaphanous the patron scent of junkies
four men in orange fluoresce
autumnal jellyfish leaning on a big wooden wheel tactile in a stone wall
step down
say 'hey you' but i am headphoned
i know they would say nothing to a man
the building is full of boxers fat guys
and slinky women
mainly it's flashy as a bright white wall pupils adjust
handstand
push up
i am the opposite of every one
each body feeling this way
about itself
climb into a machine and lift
ensuring my knees don't pass my ankles
my ancestors did work
drank beer wore sandals
i elevate heavy things and pay
like my ancestors
i love crowds

Rabid doggerel
– Georgie Spillman

In his best suit a man hauls himself onto a pyre
calling 'fire! fire! get the brigade!'
A timid onlooker (one of the canaille)
doffs her cap bowing in shame. This strange incident
she records in her notebook for our times
to adjust; scribbled back from a ragged page, to fit
meaning as needs must.

It's drag night and dresses are set to bust;
draped in recovered nylon sweet maids
fawn over tattered bustles, sovereign hems
ancient plaids. In his mother's Harvey Nicks Brocade
enters a straight boy from down shire.
Crowned sole emasculate champion,
he builds his place upon the pyre.

Within the victim, enemies multiply
'til I can't parse hate from love.
Above him flies a shadow,
the eagle that once broke
a dove. I want to take his hand in mine
just to break his fist. I must take water
to this fire,
thus his fist I kiss.

Our names are #metoo
– Ria Bhatnagar

a day to celebrate all that i am
all that they asked us not to be.

it's women's day. yet every other 364
i am taught to want to
not be like other girls.

why attach characteristics to gender?

there's nothing 'girly' about me
'boyish' about her

then our bodies. forget brains.
'i know she's a brain surgeon and stuff...
you want to grab her by the...?"

as if it's their choice to decide if a body
is worthy.
if it is

we must be so very grateful.

'what's in a name? that which we call a *rose*
by any other name would smell as sweet.'

little briar *rose* had a name.
miss sleeping... *beauty*.

ah of course, why am i not surprised?

her name - that most fundamental
form of identity - is *beauty*.

her primary value. we wonder why men still rape women and
women still learn to hate their bodies.

little briar rose was raped by her prince. a prince raped her while
she was sleeping. no / consent.

was she raped because of her name?
her *beauty*?

we read this book to little men little women alike
at half past eight before sleep, then wonder why
they have nightmares.

or worse, they have happy dreams.
we condition ourselves into thinking it's normal.
that the biggest honour bestowed upon a woman is *beauty*. the
happiest ending she could receive is
a prince raping her in her sleep.

what prince charming couldn't realise
when he kissed little briar rose
was her lips, tattooed
in menstrual blood with #metoo.

the next best compliment
'beauty with brains'

is that a rare combination?
because every woman i know
is beautiful and intelligent.

little briar rose is screaming #METOO!
you are yelling #metoo!

i am whispering #metoo.

and in that there is power

I can't sleep
– India De Bono

It's 1.35 I can't sleep
there's pain pulsating through
my veins every crevice
nodules each joint and ribs
my back is on fire
only not hot
it's an ice hurt
burning that stings
your eyes. It's 1.38 now still
I can't sleep can't
find any ibuprofen
so dihydrocodeine it is
probably better at this point
anyway
should take a sleeping tablet
too. There's no water
of course there fucking isn't
dry swallow I guess by now it's
1.42 and I am so far
from sleeping. I'm hunched over
my phone and you'd think
the position so uncomfortable it's actually
finally slinking away the medication
helping the pain… still
dull fire 1.44 just
fifteen more minutes
another 2am dawns my mind
racing but still so
exhausted. Going nonstop
since half eleven yesterday
morning my brain won't
shan't can't stop
compulsive need
just keep growing
anxieties thoughts
fears. It's 1.48
pain glowing

decided to arrive
late at the party
and wasn't even invited?
A gate-crasher of destruction
cadaver breathing still
wearing pyjamas
stop wearing my pyjamas
taking over my skin
doesn't feel like mine
this body I'm in.
Its 1.55 how time flies
shaking me back to bed
these mortal ties.

Some developments are unforeseeable
– Meg Watts

A 100-year-old man walks in circles
for the NHS; comprised of ~~saints, angels, heroes~~ MARTYRS.
I can't think about this too long.
I'll sink into a lifetime depression (like my father,
his father before him). *You can't run away
from the forces of darkness Zilpah, you can't run away
to Europe, you've got to stay and fight the good fight here.*

The politics I believe don't exist yet.
I don't want to start them; what if I become like *them*
what if it breaks me? Twisted by greed?
What if when I down my tools (with force)
they're thrown right back at me, harder?

I promised you on that hospital ward when we thought
you were dying; when we could still visit though WHO said
not to. When we didn't keep 2 metres away,
we all held your hand— if Covid got you, at least it would be over
sooner (*You know, there's such a thing as living too long*).
I held your hand I shouldn't have
held, looked in your eyes, promised

I'd stay. You couldn't die
I needed you for the revolution. You smiled,
delighted, twinkling:
you'd try the physio again tomorrow
(if you hadn't died in your sleep, *of course*)
I'd given you something to try for.

You held us all in your heart in the twinkle of your eye and said,

You've been a wonderful family.
A wonderful, hurting, disillusioned, brilliant family.
My Nana, who always saw a better future,
who asked *where can I sign up? Whose organising? Which group?*
when I first joked about socialist revolution. My Nana
would never allow herself to die

under a tory government in 2015, 2017, 2019.

Look where we are now.
We bumped elbows before we cremated you.
We got drunk in your pub and ate scones.
Your order of service, the second one, said:

Roy and Barbara were great supporters of the NHS and our other public institutions, and steadfast supporters of a fairer society and equal opportunity for all.

I hold you and your memory in power.
I draw on you for the strength to move.
It's ironic, 'young' as I am, with 'so much to live for';

I have so little left to lose.

Song for my enemies, dedicated to my parents
– Jules Chung

I am free. I insist. You cannot resist me.
You think of me as alien, a taste that's been allowed
But my roots reach far, far down; a forest does not care
Where the seeds that birthed it hail from, all it knows is light and air
Fresh and muddled, they bathed my body,
Now my trunk is thick and strong
My roots slice through bone-dryness
To draw water, Right or Wrong
Do not enter the discussion, life must live, go on and on...
Your contempt did sting at first
When I confused your thoughts for food
But as I grew I realized I must feast on all things good:
Good thoughts, good acts, good friends, good times,
Good books, good drink, good food, good rhymes,
Good fights, good days, good nights, good love
Good faith, good luck, good tears, good troubles
Good moves, good sleep--the frailty of soap bubbles.
My parents died 10,000 times and lived to give me more, much more,
To treasure, to accomplish, than they imagined or set store by.
Who am I to waste this richness? this trove? this grocery?
By dwelling in the shade, playing small, burying myself when
I am great as you are. That's all I know, the rest is din,
As I simply reach my branches out and form a canopy
By touching soft growth all around me, yours too—
Like when we made believe we were London Bridge—
You're not my enemy. You're just off centre when you see
How much I feel myself, how freely I am free.

Grey paint, gold pen
– Kiera Summer

these are different days because i'm grieving,
miraculous, midas of sorrows, our patron saint,
mother us now and at the hour of our deaths,
grief, fortuitous, grieving,
only those with the luck of imagining other worlds can,
and do,
there are lots of things I've never had,
but,
the sky is blue, I'm painting, uproot,
my carrots to find,
a three headed sprig of god, and one angry, unsubtle millipede
I am grieving still,
yes, now that I am still, it begins,
it is the noise that raises its palmed eyes to silence,
sees grey all through the air,
out the window,
into the smoke-filled autumn,
on each golden leaf,
each tired thread of hair,
every child's laughter a little grey, testing the
limits of language,
questioning how to get and keep,
saying mummy three times, to check, what is
there, and if it is words,
that can make it stay, or grief

Lower your hammer, raise your fist/song of solidarity
– Georgie Spillman

Put down your broken hammers
raise a naked fist
the stone is not the zeitgeist
but the bulwark of our shift.
Cast off your fettered glasses,
don your party kit
for better in the mines may
echo an eternal kiss.

The kiss comes back, travelling
fingers and hands: the fist of love
pervades, re-walks not its path.

So comrade come close, step
ever closer: that hope
that struggle calcify
us together; the breaths we gasp tie our feet
together. If I step forward,
so do you;
when I lose a foot, give me your shoe.

Put down broken hammers
and raise your naked fists,
For only rock can conquer fear;
regain our share, our bliss.

To die would be an awfully big adventure
– India De Bono

I went back to the place where
I nearly died.
The me I knew before
drowned in tears I never
cried
but also those I did.
I retraced the path
I once was wheeled,
using steps never touched
before. Uncanny;
half-recognised
rooms and corridors
recollected, getting lost
in labyrinths of ramps,
a collection of doors.
To face the place
that nearly killed me
to be breathing boldly still,
I think:

'To live would be an awfully big adventure'

That's a journey I want to take.

The earth rotating
– Bernard Tinashe Kuyayama

In due time, the sun rises
What stretches one's mind; the hard times

The confession
– Bernard Tinashe Kuyayama

Taste society like cocktails mixed
In a land of opportunity, my dream won't fail
In the face of adversity, my faith prevails

Spiriting
– Ofem Ubi

I know death to have a tribal mark
my skin is too thick.

I've lived archiving
deceased faces
wear my father's name
to reduce casualties
let younger blood attend older
how else to kill two birds with one stone?
nothing saps life from one destined
the vendor of happiness

watch me convert this form
a cathedral for spirits
a safe space for my father's ghost
let him roam this deputy body

stir the wisp of last breath in a cauldron
tell me they'll be a third day
after eighteen years
I am a soil of souls
a harvest of names
in these whistling decades
I am still here
drinking illumination
the moon
an intern of truth
documenting
the spirit leads.

All we have is love
– Jesse Smith

when we fuck

        the ground will shake with the smack of your hips
into mine our rocking the very earth like the dead
      are waking & layers & layers of bones that held hate for us
in the cavities of their marrow will shatter with our frequency
            that catches clouds by the throat
& fucks 'em & our love will rain over our kingdom
      from the heavens like communion wine we don't need
to age when we're the gods of the moment & when
you make me screech your name in the frequency
     of euphoria your finger on my cunt will frack
every bone down to the very cavities
       of straight love our trans hips a double-faced
moon & love is a bitter thing
    we wash our trans bodies in sweat
  over our congregants & my orgasm will belong
    to every bone & bug & crumb of soil & every

                  fucker
    who would have stamped us into
the very ground they rot in & some will want to
    die from the embarrassment of enjoying themselves
so queer there'll be no more dying 'cause

     what i feel is too good not to share

Bios

Ofem Ubi is a poet, photographer, and film maker from Nigeria, shortlisted for the Nigerian Students Poetry Prize, 2018, and published in the *Deep Dreams Anthology*. He seeks to fuse art genres into documentation, presently using film, music, poetry, and photography to tell time and archive the present.

Molly Willis is a 25-year-old writer and musician from Norwich. A graduate of the University of Warwick's English & Theatre Studies programme, her creative writing work spans personal essays, scriptwriting, and poetry.

Larry Liquid is a former inhabitant of the fine old city of Norwich, looking forward to returning post-everything. Biggest act of rebellion was selling chewing gum at high school and taking excess amounts of complimentary bus sugar.

Claudia Vyvyan is an emerging poet and playwright currently studying Education and International Development at the University of Cambridge. Her poetry has also been published in *Notes Magazine*, and she was shortlisted for the Hope Mill Theatre's Through the Mill national playwriting competition with her play, *Middle, Beginning and End*. Her upcoming radio play, *Don't Interrupt Me*, recently won the HATS new writing competition.

Nathan Lunt is a poet, performer, educator, and events organizer, currently working on publishing his first collection of poems. You can find his daily ramblings on IG @virtual_scribe

Ga-Modimo Aalim Dinake also known by the stage name The Conman/CON_scious_MAN is an individual interested in the glory of existence, using his creative craft to express his outlook and understanding of the world. From writing, to the performing arts, to drawing, and other forms, he uses his imagination to embody the emotions and feelings of mankind and tell his truth.

Haziq Patel is the author of *Stop the Killing* (Public Menace, 2021). As a British Muslim with Lancastrian roots and a product of the African/Indian diaspora, his poems and spoken word poetry are inspired by those that speak truth to power. He lives and pens from Herts to touch your hearts. Twitter @haziqpatel

Adrian Mukuvare is a creative individual with an interest in music, art, and poetry. He is of Zimbabwean origin and moved to London at the tender age of 11 in the 2000s. His move to the capital helped shape his views on socio-economic and political issues; something that was already well defined as both his parents were educators and advocates for the less fortunate in society. He currently works in financial services and mentors young people who desire to enter the professional world.

Farah is a new writer from the UK. They like to write about the lessons they have learnt through life experiences, the self, and current affairs. They find that writing offers catharsis, an opportunity to connect with others as well as widen and challenge perceived norms. IG: @tapestry_of_expression

Meg Watts (she/her): Queer writer seeks creative community to (eventually) establish eco-commune. Tells funny stories, makes bad art and says f!ck no to Capitalism. Occasionally succumbs to nihilistic despondency under crushing weight of environmental anxiety and sheer injustice of Eurocentric, heteronormative and patriarchal hegemony. Counters with activism (and sad, sexy poetry). Interested? Check @megwattscreative

Itai and Liv: Itai's a scientist who works in drug research and development. He aims to use his skills to advance wellbeing and eradicate diseases in Africa. Liv is an aspiring criminal defence lawyer. Upon graduating, she aims to provide a voice for the marginalised and young people in the criminal justice system.

Bios

Anna Bailey is a young poet and writer from the North of England. She is currently pursuing a history degree at the University of Oxford, where she balances academic work with creative pursuits. She was born in 2001.

John Swale: Described by Tim Bricheno (Sisters of Mercy) as being like 'John Cooper Clarke and W. H Auden having an all harmonicas blazing internal mic battle', John Swale has toured all over Europe, performed at major festivals, and had poems published in five publications.

Plum Selfridge (they/she) lives and writes in Scotland. She screams into the sea every Wednesday and you're always welcome to join.

Vitalis Gumbo: They live in Harare, Zimbabwe. Being creative has always been in their blood; their manuscripts include songs, short films, and poetry. As an entrepreneur in Zimbabwe's mining sector, they travel a lot which aids their creative process. They are a member of PEN Zimbabwe, helping them network with various artists, and this year, they are looking to publish their first poetry collection. The journey continues.

David Green has only been writing for two years, his poetry comes from flow-of-consciousness journaling and a need to quieten the internal monologue. As yet unpublished, he cities influences from Kae Tempest, Matt Abbott, and Salena Godden, through to Seamus Heaney, Chuck D, and Amy Winehouse. He writes on subjects including mental health, addiction, and social affairs. Find him online @BikuWandering

Sabina Redzepagic is a mother, advocate and sometimes poet...

Erica Wood: They are 19 years old, from Peterborough, currently studying Liberal Arts at Leeds University, majoring in Philosophy. Their poem, 'The Mirror', embodies their interest in feminist philosophy, particularly the works of Judith Butler, exploring the ways in which gender is performative and the subjection of the female body to disciplinary practices.

Georgie Spillman is an imprecise, genderless twenty-something, inhabiting the Norfolk Broads. It is said they spend most of their time obsessing about America: watching its bombastic downfall and mourning its forgotten dead. What is certain is that Georgie believes we need new stories about our future and present.

Ria Bhatnagar is a 16 year old student, from Bangalore, India. She believes strongly in the power of art to drive change, and aspires to spend the rest of her life engaging in creating music and poetry that tells bold and unashamed stories.

India De Bono: They are a 22-year-old student from London studying in Scotland. Diagnosed with a brain tumour in September 2020, they are currently on a year out of education. They also deal with chronic illnesses which influences their poetry. They were directed to apply for this publication when they posted the first of these poems on Twitter using the hashtag #neisvoid.

Jules Chung is a parent and the child of Korean immigrants to the US. Her work has been published in *Quince Magazine*. She writes poetry and fiction and is the recipient of the Icebox Residency with The Cabins as one-half of the creative collective, *Unattended Bags*. She is a 2021 Finalist in the *One Story* Adina Talve-Goodman Fellowship competition.

Kiera Summer is a writer of poetry and prose with a BA in French and Arabic from the University of Cambridge. She is in her second year of the MA in Creative Writing from the University of East Anglia and is currently writing to explore techno, drugs, and intergenerational temporality.

Bernard Tinashe Kuyayama: They are from Zimbabwe, 28 years old. They like poetry because it exposes their innermost emotions and interests which they might not have known were in them. They write concise poetry; the readers will expand it. Yes, they appreciate the tree leaves, the shade and the birds on the branches but they are more interested in what the roots eat that makes the tree so beautiful and habitable.

Jesse Smith is a queer poet from the UK, studying for their ma in poetry with the university of east anglia. they primarily write on gender and sexuality and their interplay with the body and with language. they have individual poems with stone of madness press and delicate friend, and one longlisted with the young poet's network. they can be found on twitter and instagram @jess_poet.

Acknowledgements and notes

This is just the first of hopefully many editions of Public Menace to come, and this collection could not have come into fruition without the collaboration and support of many people. Many thanks go out to the UEA Publishing Project at the University of East Anglia, to Jen McDerra, Nathan Hamilton, Shannon Clinton-Copeland and Polly Halladay for offering their support and time to give Public Menace the chance to be a REAL THING. Thank you to Garen Torikian and Erin Maniatopoulou for their assistance and teamwork in establishing Underdogs Alliance at UPP!

Thank you to Nigel Aono-Billson for designing the Public Menace Identity, this anthology – cover and book – and an ENORMOUS thank you to Elvis Gumbo for helping with the Public Menace website and social media – definitely couldn't have done this without you! Big love to Daisy, Zab and Flo – thank you for holding everything together. Last but certainly not least, immense gratitude to all those across the world who shared Public Menace online and responded to this submissions call. Without you, this wouldn't have been possible!

Notes:

'The World We Want Is Us'- from Alice Walker, *The World We Want Is Us*

'Because we hate you and your reason...'- Aimé Césaire, *from Notebook of a Return to my Native Land*

'We don't hold that poetry is a form of, or replaces, political action. . .'- Andrea Abi-Karam and Kay Gabriel, from *We Want It All Anthology of Transpoetics*

'Take Root Among the Stars'- Octavia Butler, *Parable of the Sower*

'All Shall Be Well'- St Julian of Norwich, *Revelations of Divine Love*